The Eyeball
Alphabet Book

Jerry Pallotta

Shennen Bersani

Charlesbridge

Dear Reader,
These fish eyeballs are looking at you.
And guess what? Your eyeballs are looking
at them. How do eyeballs work? We are
going to find out. Also look for an *eye idiom*
on every page. An idiom is an expression
that means something different from what
it actually says.

To Katherine, Leigh, John, and Jimmy Colihan—J. P.

To my daughter Karlene and son-in-law Patrick
in honor of their big day, August 23—S. B.

Published by Charlesbridge
9 Galen Street
Watertown, MA 02472
(617) 926-0329
www.charlesbridge.com

Printed in China
(hc) 10 9 8 7 6 5 4 3 2 1

Illustrations done in Prismacolor pencils on Arches
    watercolor paper and manipulated in Photoshop
Title type set in Cafeteria © The Font Bureau,
    by Tobias Frere-Jones
Text type set in Gotham by Hoefler & Frere-Jones
Printed by 1010 Printing International Limited in Huizhou,
    Guangdong, China
Production supervision by Jennifer Most Delaney
Designed by Cathleen Schaad

Library of Congress Cataloging-in-Publication Data
Names: Pallotta, Jerry, author. | Bersani, Shennen, illustrator.
Title: The eyeball alphabet book / Jerry Pallotta ; illustrated
    by Shennen Bersani.
Description: Watertown, MA : Charlesbridge, [2021] |
    Summary: "This alphabet book about animals and their
    eyes has an idiom that includes the word 'eye' on every
    page"— Provided by publisher.
Identifiers: LCCN 2020000772 (print) | LCCN 2020000773
    (ebook) | ISBN 9781570917103 (hardcover) | ISBN
    9781632896124 (ebook)
Subjects: LCSH: Eye—Juvenile literature. | Animals—
    Miscellanea—Juvenile literature. | Animals—
    Adaptation—Juvenile literature. | Alphabet books—
    Juvenile literature. | Alphabet—Juvenile literature.
Classification: LCC QL949 .P35 2021 (print) | LCC
    QL949 (ebook) | DDC 591.4/4—dc23
LC record available at https://lccn.loc.gov/
    2020000772
LC ebook record available at https://lccn.loc.gov/
    2020000773

A is for **Alligator.** An alligator has eyes that stick up on the top of its head. It can look above the water while the rest of its head and body are hidden below the water.

Aa

Keep your eye on the ball
means to pay attention.

Bb

B is for **Bay Scallop**. A bay scallop is a small clam. Look! It has lots of eyes. Blue eyes! A scallop's eyes help it locate food.

To have stars in your eyes means that you want to be famous.

C is for **Camel.** Human beings have one eyelid on each eye that opens and closes. The camel has two types of moveable eyelids on each eye. One type goes up and down and blocks light. The other type is clear and goes from side to side. This allows the camel to see and protect its eyes while walking in a sandstorm.

Cc

In the blink of an eye **means that something happens fast.**

Dd

D is for **Dog.** This husky has one blue eye and one brown eye. In the animal kingdom, most creatures have eyes that are the same color. Think of your friends. Do you know anyone with one brown eye and one blue eye? Only about six of every one thousand people have different-colored eyes.

To keep an eye out for something **means to be alert and aware.**

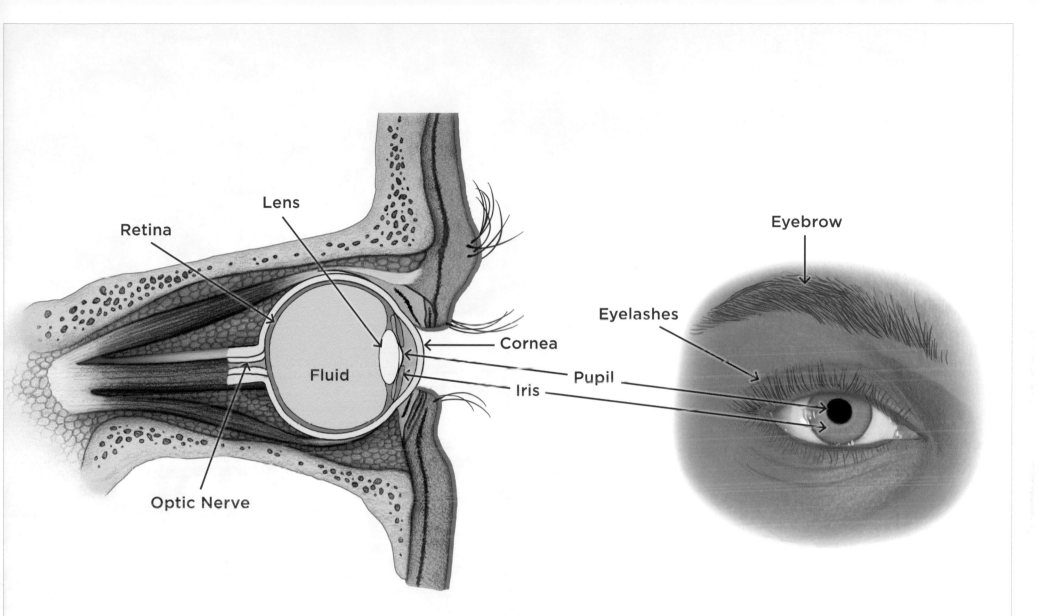

Retina

Lens

Optic Nerve

Fluid

Cornea

Pupil

Iris

Eyebrow

Eyelashes

How does an eye work? First, you need light. Light reflects off the back of your eyeball, the retina. The retina converts the light into a signal. The signal is sent through the optic nerve to your brain. Your brain shows the image, and you can see!

To be a hawkeye means to be good at noticing things around you.

Ee

E is for **Eel.** This eel's eyes are camouflaged. Its eyes look like the spots around them. Eels and most other fish do not have movable eyelids. Their eyes are always open. This cleaner shrimp has blue eyes on short stalks. Cleaner shrimp have terrible eyesight, but they still manage to clean fishes' and other animals' mouths!

In the eye of a storm **means to be in the center of a difficult situation.**

F is for **Frog.** Frog eyes come in all different designs and colors. It doesn't matter what color its eyes are. It's how well it sees that counts. Most frogs have bulging eyes that allow them to see in front, to the sides, and partially behind them. Don't you wish you could do that?

Ff

To have an eagle eye means to notice all the details.

Ff

Just for fun, here is another F.

F is also for **Fly.**

This is a common housefly. Flies are hard to catch because their eyes are expert at sensing movement. They have compound eyes. The red you see here is not just one eye but thousands of individual eyes.

Swat! We missed again.

A *sight for sore eyes* means someone or something you are happy to see.

G is for **Giant Squid.** The giant squid has the largest eyeballs in the world. Each eye is about the size of a basketball. That's bigger than your head! The giant squid's huge eyes allow it to see better in the deep, dark ocean.

To be in the public eye means **to be known and talked about by many people.**

Hh

H is for **Horse.** People have eyes with round pupils. A horse has eyes with oval-shaped pupils. A horse can use monocular vision, which means each eye sees something different. A horse can also see to the side in a panoramic view, but not straight ahead.

Get some shut-eye
means to get some sleep.

I is for **Indri.** The Indri is a lemur. It has large, greenish eyes. In some cultures, people will not look at a lemur. It is considered an evil omen.

When an animal's eyes are in front, it is called binocular vision. Each eye is looking at the same image. Binocular vision allows you to judge distance. This ability is called depth perception.

To give someone the evil eye means to wish bad things will happen to them.

Ii

Jj

J is for **Jaguar.** You are looking at a predator, which is an animal that hunts other animals. Here is a rhyme about predators and prey, which are animals that are hunted: "Eyes in front, likes to hunt. Eyes on side, likes to hide." If an animal's eyes are in front, it is usually a hunter. If an animal has eyes on the side of its head, it usually is hunted. Humans have eyes in front.

To have eyes in the back of your head means to know everything that's going on around you.

K is for **Kei Flying Fox**, a megabat. Bats have fine eyesight, and they also have sonar, which is a way to "see" with sound. The bat makes sounds and listens to the echoes. The echoes come back, giving the bat an idea of what is around it.

Kk

To see eye to eye **means to agree.**

L is for **Lobster.** Lobsters have eyes, but they can't see well. They notice only light and dark. Their antennae allow them to feel motion and vibrations in the water.

To turn a blind eye means to not care about something.

M is for **Macaw.** Birds such as macaws can see better than humans because they can see more kinds of light, such as ultraviolet.

Mm

To be able to do something with your eyes closed means to perform the task really well.

Nn

N is for **Night Crawler.** Night crawler is another name for an earthworm. Earthworms have no eyes. They never need to visit an eye doctor! An optometrist tests your vision. An optician fits you for glasses or contact lenses. An ophthalmologist is a doctor who specializes in eyes.

A private eye is slang for an undercover investigator.

Oo

O is for **Ostrich**. Ostriches have the largest eyes of any land animal. If an animal has trouble seeing things far away, it is called nearsighted. If it has trouble seeing things up close, it is farsighted. People who are nearsighted or farsighted can have their vision corrected with glasses or contact lenses. Having no eyesight is called blindness.

To keep your eyes peeled **means to look carefully for something.**

Look at these kooky glasses! Most glasses have lenses that help you see better.

Feast your eyes means to look at with pleasure.

P is for **Python.** A python can not only see you with its eyes but can also detect your heat with its thermal sensors. A thermal sensor, or pit organ, is a different way of "seeing." Another kind of snake, called a pit viper, also has thermal sensors.

Pp

Without batting an eye **means to do something without thinking much about it.**

Qq

Q is for **Quoll.** Marsupials are mammals with pouches. The quoll is a small marsupial. When a hungry hawk, python, or crocodile is hunting, a quoll may wish it had radar. But animals have no radar, which is an electronic tool that lets people see far away.

In the eye of the beholder means that everyone has their own opinion.

R is for **Rhinoceros.** A white rhinoceros is the second-largest land mammal. A rhinoceros has small eyes and poor eyesight. It makes up for its low vision with great hearing. Its ears can turn and listen in different directions.

Rr

To have a black eye means to have a damaged reputation.

Ss

S is for **Spider.** Many kids know that spiders have eight legs. But did you also know that most spiders have eight eyes? Imagine a human being with eight eyes!

An eye for an eye **means that if someone does something to you, you do the same to them. Not always a good idea!**

Tt

T is for **Tarsier.** The tarsier is holding a tarsier skull. Look how big the eye sockets are. This type of animal is rare. Each of its eyes is bigger than its brain.

Apple of your eye means something is your favorite.

Uu

U is for **Uakari**. A uakari is a monkey. This uakari's eyes are aligned, which means they are looking at the same object. Most eyes are aligned correctly, but some are not. If a right eye looks left and a left eye looks right, it is called cross-eyed. If both eyes look outward, it is called walleyed.

A red-eye is an overnight flight on an airplane.

Vv

V is for Vulture. Imagine being a bird, flying around seeing everything from above. Vultures can spot a carcass from high in the sky. They circle above it, and other vultures join for the feast.

Bird's-eye view means seen from above.

Ww

W is for **Widemouth Blindcat.** This fish lives in dark caves. It has no eyes. It doesn't need eyes, because there is no light. Jellyfish, sea urchins, blind salamanders, Mexican tetras, and yeti crabs are other animals that have no eyes.

Eyes bigger than your stomach means you think you can eat more than you actually can.

Xx

X is for **Xenosaur.** We used our eyes to search high and low for an animal that begins with the letter X. A xenosaur is from China. Its name sounds like a dinosaur, but it's a lizard. Another type of lizard, a chameleon, can move its eyes independently of each other.

Another pair of eyes **means help from someone else.**

Yy

Y is for **Yellow Fiddler Crab.** Its eyes are on long stalks. This crab can look all the way around. We call this 360-degree vision.

Pull the wool over their eyes means to fool someone.

Zz

Z is for **Zebu.** A zebu is a type of cattle. This zebu has moths in its eyes that are drinking its tears. Oops, we forgot to mention tears in this book. There are three types of tears. Some protect your eyes, some clean your eyes, and some tears happen when you cry.

To open your eyes means to become aware of something.

We end this book with a sheepdog. It can see you, but you can't see its eyes.

Take good care of your eyes!

- Wear protective equipment, such as safety goggles, for hobbies and sports.

- Avoid staring at bright light, such as the sun.

- If something gets in your eye, don't rub it.

- Get regular eye checkups.

We hope this book was an *eye-opener!*